THE QUEEN'S CORONATION

1953

THE QUEEN'S CORONATION

1953

Caroline de Guitaut

ROYAL COLLECTION TRUST

INTRODUCTION

Therefore, to Thee, all-glorious, let us pray
For her, Thy destined, consecrate today.
We, then, beseech Thee, everlasting power,
That this, Thy dedicated soul, may reign
In peace, in wisdom, for her mortal hour,
In this beloved land . . .

from *A Prayer for a Beginning Reign*,
John Masefield, Poet Laureate

The exterior of Westminster Abbey in preparation for the Coronation, from *The Place of Crowning*, illustrations by Henry Rushbury, 1953
RCIN 1057573

On 28 April 1952 it was announced from Buckingham Palace that The Queen was pleased to appoint 2 June 1953 to be the day of her Coronation. It would be held at Westminster Abbey – the royal church of the Palace of Westminster, where every coronation for the last 900 years had taken place. Queen Elizabeth II would become the thirty-ninth Sovereign and sixth queen to be crowned in her own right at Westminster Abbey.

Such was the degree of planning and preparation required that the event would take place almost 18 months after The Queen had acceded to the

throne, following the death of her father King George VI on 6 February 1952. The announcement came after three months of court mourning, leaving insufficient time in 1952 to arrange and accommodate the numerous official coronation festivities, which had been established at the time of Edward VII's coronation in 1902. For the 1937 coronation of King George VI and Queen Elizabeth, the coronation festivities had extended over almost two months.

The Coronation of Queen Elizabeth II has been seen as one of the most significant occasions in the modern life of the country, ushering in a new age of progress and a spirit of optimism in the wake of continued austerity in post-war Britain.

For those who witnessed the ceremony at Westminster Abbey, it was an unforgettable experience. Sir Henry ('Chips') Channon, the American-born Conservative MP, noted in his diaries, 'What a day for England and the traditional forces of the world. Shall we ever see the like again?'

The ceremony and spectacle were a focus for great celebration, with three million people lining the processional route in London and many others taking part in church services and attending street parties around the country. It was also enormously significant from the point of view of journalism and broadcasting. An estimated 27 million – over half the population – viewed the coronation service on television. This was the first time that a coronation ceremony had been televised and for many, it was their first experience of television. A further 11 million people listened to the radio broadcast. There were more than 2,000 journalists and 500 photographers representing 92 nations on the Coronation route, filing copy and sending newsreel to a worldwide audience.

The Organisation of the Coronation

A vast machinery of organisation was put in place to create one of the most memorable events in twentieth-century British history. The Coronation Commission was appointed in April 1952 to consider those aspects of the arrangements for the Coronation that were of common concern for the Commonwealth. Chaired by The Duke of Edinburgh, it consisted of representatives of the United Kingdom, Canada, Australia, New Zealand, South Africa, Pakistan and Ceylon. On 6 June 1952, Garter Principal King of Arms proclaimed Coronation Day from St James's Palace. The Royal Proclamation was sent to all the Colonial and Dominion governments. On the same day, the Coronation Committee, appointed by the Coronation Commission and made up of Privy Councillors, was charged with overseeing the planning of every aspect of this extraordinarily complex event.

(above) The Earl Marshal (left) with the Minister of Works and Garter Principal King of Arms studying plans of Westminster Abbey
RCIN 2587033

(facing) View of the Peeresses Gallery in the North Transept, from *The Place of Crowning*, illustrations by Henry Rushbury, 1953
RCIN 1057573

The masterminding of each component of the Coronation – liturgical, ceremonial and logistical – required expertise, skill, discretion and extraordinary vision. One of the first acts of the Coronation Committee was to form an executive committee consisting of the Earl Marshal and the Archbishop of Canterbury. The office of Earl Marshal, one of the great Offices of State, has been held by the Dukes of Norfolk since 1386; in 1953 the post was held by Bernard Fitzalan-Howard. He was responsible for making all the non-

liturgical arrangements for the Coronation, including issuing invitations to the 9,003 guests, of whom 8,251 accepted. The Earl Marshal, who set up a special office at 14 Belgrave Square in order to direct operations efficiently, had already planned the coronation of King George VI in 1937.

Another key figure in the planning and preparations for the Coronation was the Minister of Works, David Eccles, who was responsible for the logistical arrangements. For example, in order to accommodate the large number of guests, the seating capacity of Westminster Abbey had to be increased by over 5,000, a task that took more than six months to accomplish.

On 1 January 1953, five months before Coronation Day, Westminster Abbey closed completely to allow the huge task of its transformation to take place. An annexe needed to be constructed at the entrance to provide space for the processions to assemble and for the laying out of the regalia. The processional route had to be planned and seating constructed along its length in specially built stands totalling 43 kilometres. Decorations for the route had to be designed and made, flowers had to be grown and prepared, and floodlighting and fireworks had to be planned and supplied.

Pakistan troops mounting guard at Buckingham Palace, 1953
RCIN 2587149

Then there was the task of accommodating everyone in London. The 29,200 British, Colonial and Commonwealth troops who took part in the Coronation processions, including some who mounted guard at Buckingham Palace, needed to be billeted, and among the 8,251 guests attending the Coronation were Heads of State from 73 countries, all of whom had to be accommodated in London and transported to the Abbey on Coronation Day.

At Buckingham Palace, a Household Coronation Committee was set up to consider arrangements for and expenditure on the Coronation. Virtually every member of The Queen's Household played their part in some capacity or another, notably all the most senior office-holders who, as well as being deeply involved in the preparations, also undertook their traditional roles at the ceremony itself.

The Private Secretary's Office, the Master of the Household's Department and the Lord Chamberlain's Office played a central role. Their responsibilities included planning the extraordinarily full diary of Coronation engagements for The Queen and The Duke of Edinburgh, which stretched from 28 May to 10 July, procuring everything required (the official materials, such as the regalia and furnishings stipulated by the Earl Marshal in his Warrants, or official orders), arranging for the Imperial State Crown to be adjusted for The Queen, planning the order of precedence for the carriage processions, growing flowers in the royal gardens and organising numerous receptions and lunches as well as two Coronation State Banquets. In addition, The Queen herself and The Duke of Edinburgh were involved in much of the decision-making.

The coronation ritual has changed little since the earliest detailed account of the crowning of the Anglo-Saxon king, Edgar, in 973. The ceremony has six principal stages:

- The Recognition, during which the people acclaim the new Sovereign

- The Oath, by which the Sovereign pledges to serve the people

- The Anointing, an act of consecration when the Sovereign is anointed with oil on the hands, breast and head

- The Investiture, when the Sovereign is presented with the symbols of sovereignty, culminating in the Crowning

- The Homage, during which the Church and the peerage pledge their loyalty

- The Communion, during which the Sovereign receives the sacramental bread and wine.

In 1953, the Archbishop of Canterbury, Dr Geoffrey Fisher, was responsible for planning the detailed liturgy with the help of an advisory committee and in consultation with The Queen and the Duke of Edinburgh. He had presided at their wedding at Westminster Abbey in 1947. The Duke of Edinburgh was anxious to modernise some aspects of the service 'to make them relevant to the modern world' but in the event there were few innovations and the service followed that of 1937 in most of its essentials.

Dr Fisher was also responsible for preparing The Queen for the Coronation and to that end he produced a book of prayers and private devotions for her

*A little book of private
devotions in preparation for
Her Majesty's Coronation,
given by the Archbishop
of Canterbury to
The Queen, 1953*
RCIN 1006833

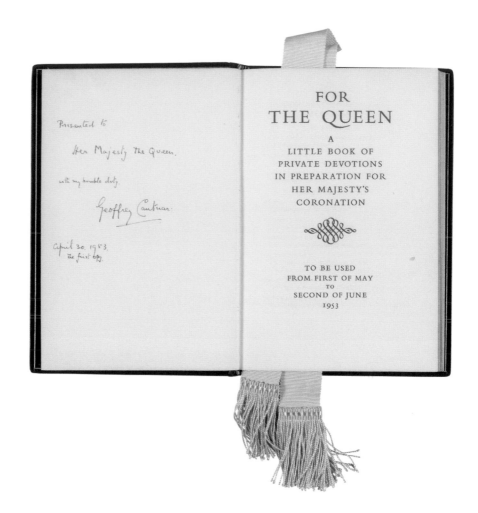

Presented to

Her Majesty the Queen.

with my humble duty.

Geoffrey Cantuar:

April 30, 1953.
the first copy.

FOR
THE QUEEN
A
LITTLE BOOK OF
PRIVATE DEVOTIONS
IN PREPARATION FOR
HER MAJESTY'S
CORONATION

TO BE USED
FROM FIRST OF MAY
TO
SECOND OF JUNE
1953

for each day of the month leading up to Coronation Day. In The Queen's first Christmas broadcast of her reign in December 1952, she had asked the people for their support and to pray for her on the day of her Coronation.

Many previous coronations had not gone as smoothly as they might have done: for example, at Queen Victoria's coronation in 1838, numerous mistakes were made by the clergy, due partly to there not having been a rehearsal. In 1953 the Earl Marshal was anxious that all should go according to plan, particularly in view of the BBC's live televising of the event. Rehearsals of

The clergy rehearsing for the procession of the regalia at Westminster Abbey, London, 23 May 1953
RCIN 2584757

(above)
The Queen leaving
Westminster Abbey with the
Duchess of Norfolk after a
rehearsal,
21 May 1953

(right)
Maids of Honour leaving
Westminster Abbey after
attending the final rehearsal of
the Coronation Ceremony,
28 May 1953

all aspects of the ceremony were therefore arranged, including a final dress rehearsal witnessed by 1,100 invited guests. Among these guests was Cecil Beaton (1904–80), who was to take the official photographic portraits on Coronation Day. The Queen herself rehearsed in private at Buckingham Palace but she also attended several rehearsals at the Abbey.

TRADITION and MODERNITY

Planning and Designing the Coronation

Arranging a spectacular Coronation in 1953 was a particular challenge given the lack of resources after the war and the exhausted state of much of London, where a great deal of bomb damage still remained. However, it was vital to create and capture an inspiring and lasting image of contemporary monarchy and provide a memorable beginning to the new reign.

Thanks to the creativity of several leading artistic figures, the Coronation was conceived in great splendour. The Earl Marshal and the Minister of Works set about finding the architects, designers, sculptors, artists and composers who would come together to produce an event of imagination and flair. Their work would encompass the ceremony itself, the decorations and constructions at Westminster Abbey, the decoration of the processional route and the entertainment of the many hundreds of dignitaries from around the world who would descend on London. The scheme would be fitting for what many, particularly in the press, began to refer to as the 'new Elizabethan era'.

The Festival of Britain in 1951, with its strong Modernist feel, had demonstrated great British innovation in the fields of architecture and design. The Coronation followed in its wake but would be a quite different cultural event:

it needed to evoke the tradition and continuity of monarchy, while at the same time looking forward to the future reign of a young queen.

In planning the Coronation, the Minister of Works, David Eccles, said that, 'it is our duty to express in colour and design the age we live in and The Queen who is to be crowned'. His approach proved key to reinforcing the idea of combining ancient rite with modern flair.

Designs for Coronation street decorations for Hungerford bridge, (above) and Whitehall (right), Hugh Casson, 1953

Sir Hugh Casson (1910–99) had come to prominence with his appointment as Director of Architecture for the Festival of Britain, for which he was knighted in 1952. For the Coronation he was tasked with designing street decorations for the principal areas of the processional route, including The Mall, Trafalgar Square, Piccadilly and Whitehall. To complement Casson's designs, Eric Bedford, the Ministry of Works' chief architect and chief designer for the Coronation, devised four huge tubular steel and wire-mesh triumphal arches, which were placed along the length of The Mall. These were painted blue and gold and were floodlit at night. The arches were surmounted by gold and silver lions and white unicorns, which raised their total height to 26 metres and a princess's coronet was suspended on wires from the centre of each arch.

One of the most strikingly modern designs prepared for the Coronation was Eric Bedford's scheme for the annexe, built at the west front of Westminster Abbey. The annexe was required not only for the assembly of the processions into the Abbey but also for the regalia to be laid out in

Eric Bedford's decorations in place on The Mall as crowds watch the procession to Buckingham Palace on Coronation Day, 2 June 1953 advance of the ceremony. In addition, it provided retiring rooms for the Royal Family and it was where lunch would be served to the immediate royal party after the Coronation ceremony and before The Queen's procession set off on its return to Buckingham Palace (see p. 25).

For several earlier coronations, the temporary structures built for this purpose around the Abbey had tended to be of pseudo-Gothic design, in keeping with the Abbey's own architectural language. For the 1953 Coronation, however, Bedford's design was uncompromisingly modern and angular, with a lofty and elegant interior. It was, nonetheless, embellished with more traditional decorative elements including glass engraved with national emblems and exterior adornments consisting of ten Queen's beasts – heraldic animals depicting The Queen's genealogy – designed by the sculptor James Woodford RA (1893–1976). The two-metre-high heraldic beasts made of clay and plaster were intended to be temporary, however after the Coronation they were moved to Hampton Court Palace for display in the Great Hall. They were temporarily relocated to St George's Hall at Windsor Castle, and in 1959 were offered to the Canadian government. They are now in the care of the Canadian Museum of Civilisation in Quebec. Copies made from Portland stone, produced by James Woodford in 1958, are now located in the Royal Botanical Gardens at Kew in London.

Inside the Abbey, the Coronation Theatre was created in the Sacrarium and the dais was erected for the throne chair. The Queen was closely consulted over furnishings for the Coronation Theatre, including the Chair of Estate used in the first part of the service and the Throne Chair, where she would be enthroned after the crowning.

(left)
Eric Bedford's modernist
annexe at Westminster Abbey,
30 May 1953

(below)
Six of the ten Queen's Beasts
outside the Abbey annexe,
29 May 1953

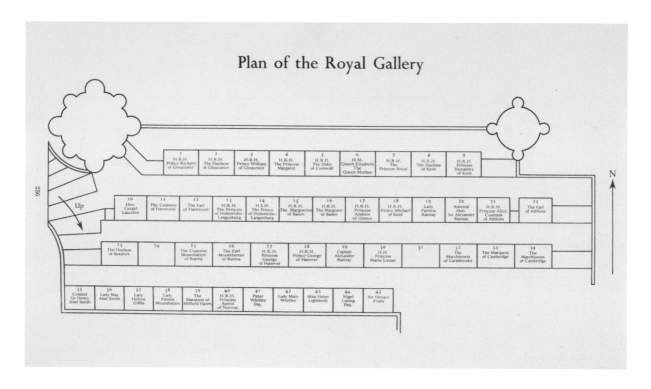

Plan of the Royal Gallery

N

Up

Coronation Furnishings

At first the intention had been to reuse as many of the ceremonial furnishings made for King George VI's coronation as possible. In 1952, Mr Barker from the Ministry of Works wrote to the Lord Chamberlain's Office to say that the Earl Marshal had informed him that it would not be necessary to make new ceremonial chairs and stools, as in most cases, those used in 1937 could be renovated and reused. In the event, however, a new Throne Chair, Chair of Estate and five faldstools, or prie-dieux, were made.

The seating plan for the Royal Gallery, Westminster Abbey
RA-LC-LCO-COR-1953

Queensway, designed by
Robert Goodden, woven by
Warner & Sons, 1952

Vast quantities of furnishings were required for the guests. These included 2,000 peers' chairs made of oak and beech, upholstered in blue velour trimmed with gold braid, and with the royal cipher embossed on the back. In keeping with tradition, these were offered for sale afterwards (chairs cost £7 10s 0d and stools £4 7s 6d), with preference given to offers from those who had occupied them.

The chairs used by Queen Elizabeth The Queen Mother, Princess Margaret and Prince Charles, then known as The Duke of Cornwall, who were seated in the Royal Gallery, were sent to Windsor Castle after the Coronation.

On 21 January 1953, David Eccles wrote to the Lord Chamberlain to inform him that there was good progress with the designs for the decorations of the Abbey but it was taking longer to produce everything due to high levels of employment. In addition to the chairs, new carpets and some new damask frontals to decorate the temporary galleries inside the Abbey were required. After many trials, Eccles accepted a design for the frontals by Professor Robert Goodden (1909–2002) of the Royal College of Art. This design, in blue and gold, was approved by The Queen on 26 January.

A new altar frontal was also produced specially for the Coronation and this is still in use on occasions at Westminster Abbey. The silk panels embroidered with the Royal Arms, used to decorate the royal galleries and the regalia table of the annexe, were partly reused from the 1937 coronation. After the 1953 Coronation, applications could be made for the purchase of the carpets and the damask frontals made for the temporary galleries, with preference given to applications received from churches.

Coronation Flowers

One of Eccles' notable appointments was to engage Constance Spry (1886–1960), the leading floral designer, to decorate the processional route with flowers and to act as honorary consultant on floral decoration. As her biographer Sue Shepherd indicates, Spry was not necessarily a popular choice with the senior figures at the Ministry of Works but she won them over with her professionalism, knowledge and flair. Moreover, she had already been entrusted with designing and preparing the flowers for Princess Elizabeth's wedding at Westminster Abbey in 1947.

Her advice on the colour and style of the flowers lining the processional route, which was decorated with banks of flowers in blocks and drifts of scarlet, pale blue and gold, was crucial to their visual success, not only in situ but most particularly on television. Spry also suggested reinforcing the usual scheme of red geraniums around the Monument to Queen Victoria in front of Buckingham Palace by adding red verbenas and red salvias, and she designed parterres of soft pinks and mauves for outside the Abbey annexe to evoke an English country garden in high summer.

Four hectares of flowers had to be grown in the greenhouses of the Royal Parks to bloom on exactly the right day and these were richly supplemented by contributions of plants and flowers from Commonwealth countries including Australia, India and South Africa, and by the colonial territories of Bermuda, Hong Kong, Jamaica, Malaya, Malta, Northern Rhodesia, Trinidad and Tobago, Sierra Leone and Singapore. Orchids sent by Singapore were used in the Abbey in the Queen's Robing Room and at Lancaster House, where a Coronation banquet also designed by Spry was given by the Secretary of State for Foreign Affairs.

Constance Spry's role extended to organising the post-Coronation luncheon for 350 dignitaries from around the world, who were to be entertained in the Great Hall of Westminster School. Not only did she produce a highly imaginative decorative scheme for the luncheon in gold, blue and scarlet, but this was the occasion for which her colleague, Rosemary Hume, invented *Poulet Reine Elizabeth*, more popularly known as Coronation Chicken. Made with strips of cold chicken in a light curry-flavoured sauce, the dish was inspired by the favourite recipe of Queen Adelaide, consort of William IV. The luncheon was served by students from Winkfield Place, Spry's cookery school, who wore outfits designed by the couturier Victor Stiebel.

Constance Spry's floral and decorative schemes for many of the elements of the Coronation revealed her ingenious solutions to the shortage of raw materials in 1953. She also helped with designing the colour scheme of the banners in front of Buckingham Palace and along the processional route, which featured The Queen's cipher picked out in gold on a red background.

Invitations

The wood engraver and book illustrator Joan Hassall (1906–88), was to play an important role in the Coronation preparations. Hassall was a successful book illustrator and in 1948 had designed the £1 postage stamp issued to

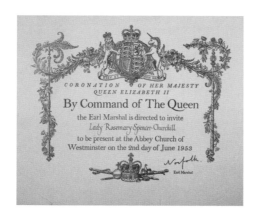 

(left)
Invitation sent to Lady Rosemary Spencer-Churchill, one of The Queen's Maids of Honour. The design incorporates the Royal Arms, national and commonwealth emblems, Joan Hassall, 1953

(right)
Invitation for Prince Charles, Duke of Cornwall, to attend the Coronation of Queen Elizabeth II, Joan Hassall, 1953
RCIN 452424

commemorate the silver wedding of King George VI and Queen Elizabeth. To add to these successes, in 1953 she won the competition to design the official invitation to the 1953 Coronation, an invitation that was traditionally issued in the name of the Earl Marshal.

Hassall usually worked as a wood engraver but there was not enough time to produce a wood engraving for the large and complex design of the Coronation invitation, so she had to use scraperboard instead.

In addition to the official invitation, Hassall also designed the personal invitation that The Duke of Cornwall received to the Coronation. This charming design reveals the meticulous observation and skill that were hallmarks of Hassall's work.

Coronation Music

Music has played a vitally important role at coronations over the centuries, but particularly at the three preceding coronations in the twentieth century. On those occasions it provided a festival of music on a grand scale, designed to fit the importance of the occasion and engender patriotism and pride. The music required careful rehearsal and immaculate timing and for the 1953 Coronation the role of music director was entrusted to William McKie, organist and master of the choristers at Westminster Abbey.

The music for The Queen's Coronation was a combination of the preordained and the newly composed. The anthem *I Was Glad* (a setting of Psalm 122), first composed in 1902 for Edward VII's coronation by Sir Hubert Parry (1848–1914), was used during the monarch's entry procession, just as it had been at the three preceding coronations. Handel's anthem *Zadok the Priest*,

written for the coronation of George II in 1727 and used at every coronation since, was sung during the Anointing.

Among the nine newly composed pieces was the anthem O *Taste and See How Gracious the Lord Is* by Ralph Vaughan Williams (1872–1958), which was sung during the Communion. Vaughan Williams was also responsible for suggesting that the congregation might participate by singing, and for this purpose he made a special arrangement of the hymn *All People that on Earth do Dwell*. This was the congregation's only act apart from the moment of Acclamation immediately after the Crowning, when the peers and peeresses put on their coronets.

Another new piece of music was by the Canadian composer, Healey Willan, who wrote an anthem O *Lord our Governor*, which was sung during

The Queen and
The Duke of Edinburgh
at the premiere of
the opera *Gloriana*,
8 June 1953
RCIN 2002638

the Homage. Traditionally, the *Te Deum*, sung after the monarch was crowned, was given a new setting at each coronation and in 1953 this was undertaken by Sir William Walton (1902–83), who also composed the orchestral piece *Orb and Sceptre*. In addition, Sir Arnold Bax (1883–1953) composed a coronation march, which was played after Elgar's *Pomp and Circumstance*.

The combined choirs of Westminster Abbey, St Paul's Cathedral, the Chapel Royal and St George's Chapel, Windsor, together with representatives from The Queen's Chapel of the Savoy, the Chapel Royal, Hampton Court Palace and the Chapel of St Peter ad Vincula at the Tower of London all sang at The Queen's Coronation. In total the choir numbered 400 voices supplemented by 60 orchestral players.

The composer Benjamin Britten (1913–76) did not contribute any music to the Coronation ceremony itself, but instead composed the three-act opera *Gloriana*, specially commissioned by the Royal Opera House to mark the Coronation. For this service, Britten was appointed a Companion of Honour. The libretto by Willam Plomer tells the story of the relationship between Queen Elizabeth I and the Earl of Essex. The production was designed by the artist John Piper (1903–92) and the set decoration was by Oliver Messel (1904–78).

The Queen, The Duke of Edinburgh and many other members of the Royal Family attended the premiere at Covent Garden on 8 June as part of the series of official Coronation festivities. The opera received poor reviews and has not been staged again by the Royal Opera House until its revival in 2013, marking the sixtieth anniversary of the Coronation.

MAGNIFICENT FINERY

Dressing for the Coronation

The conspicuous display of rich dress worn by kings and queens at coronations is a tradition that dates back over many centuries. The succession of imperial and sacred garments worn by the sovereign during a coronation has changed little since the seventeenth century. In fact, the order of coronation dress refers back to the *Liber Regalis*, a fourteenth-century illuminated manuscript which has provided the basis for the order of service of all coronations since 1382.

The king or queen arrives for the procession into Westminster Abbey wearing the crimson Parliamentary Robe, also known as the Robe of State. The monarch is then divested of this robe and is anointed, after which he or she puts on a plain white sleeveless linen shift known as the *Colobium Sindonis*, followed by the *Supertunica* or the Close Pall of cloth of gold. Next the Stole Royal is placed around the monarch's neck before he or she is dressed in the Imperial Mantle, also known as the Robe Royal. Finally, for the procession out of the Abbey, the newly crowned Sovereign wears the purple Robe of Estate, also known as the Coronation Robe.

Tradition also dictates the attire for many of those witnessing or taking part in the coronation ceremony. By tradition, the Earl Marshal updates the rules governing dress and seeks the sovereign's approval for the changes. In

1953 much consideration was given to ensuring that those who had the right to attend the Coronation should not be prevented from being able to dress correctly because of the expense of costly new robes or other elements of dress. Thus, when the Earl Marshal came to update the rules, economy of design was as important as availability of materials.

The Queen's Coronation Dress

A newly designed Coronation dress has been produced for all queens regnant or consort, over which, for queens regnant, the sacred garments of investiture – *Colobium Sindonis*, *Supertunica* and Imperial Mantle – are placed. Over the centuries, a queen's coronation dress has become memorable through its depiction in official state portraits, both painted and photographic, produced at the start of the reign. The design of coronation dresses in the twentieth century involved not only rich fabrics and embellishments, particularly embroideries, but also evolving iconography.

In October 1952, the couturier, Norman Hartnell (1901–79), was entrusted with the task of designing The Queen's Coronation Dress. Hartnell had great experience of designing for royal ceremonial occasions: his first major commission as a royal couturier had been to design the dresses worn by the Maids of Honour to Queen Elizabeth at the 1937 coronation. He subsequently became principal Designer By Appointment to Queen Elizabeth designing the majority of her wardrobe until his death in 1979. Hartnell began to design for Princess Elizabeth from the early 1940s, his most notable commission being for the Princess's wedding dress in 1947. By the time of The Queen's

(left)
Queen Mary in Coronation Robes, Sir William Samuel Henry Llewellyn, 1912
RCIN 402024

(right)
Queen Elizabeth in Coronation Robes, Sir Gerald Festus Kelly, 1945
RCIN 403423

accession in 1952, he was her principal designer and his talent for combining rich fabrics and exquisitely designed embroideries with both modern cuts and classically inspired lines made him the obvious choice to produce the most important dress of The Queen's reign. According to Hartnell's own account in his memoir, *Silver and Gold*, The Queen indicated that the coronation dress should conform to the line of her wedding dress and that the material should be of white satin. This gave Hartnell a relatively free rein and he set about his painstaking research to study coronation dresses of earlier queens, notably, according to his own account, those of Queen Elizabeth I, Queen Anne and Queen Victoria. He thought of 'altar clothes and sacred vestments … and everything heavenly that might be embroidered upon a dress destined to be historic'.

Hartnell prepared nine differing designs ranging from the simple to the more elaborate which he submitted for The Queen's consideration. The first was a very simple design in white satin with light embroidery recalling Queen Victoria's coronation dress; the second was on a more modern line with gold embroidery and ermine trim; the third was a crinoline shape with silver and crystal embroidery; the fourth was inspired by the theme of the Madonna; the fifth incorporated coloured embroideries; the sixth again of white satin had gold embroideries of oak leaves; the seventh incorporated the Tudor Rose of England.

The eighth design had silver embroidery that extended the idea of the Tudor Rose of England to include the other three national emblems – the thistle (for Scotland), the shamrock (for Ireland) and the daffodil (for Wales). This was very similar to the design that would finally be chosen.

The Queen was pleased with the eighth design but suggested that the embroideries were executed in various colours (as in the fifth design) rather than all in silver, which were close to the colour scheme of her wedding dress. In response to The Queen's suggestions, Hartnell worked up the ninth and final design. At a subsequent audience, The Queen requested of Hartnell that the four national emblems be supplemented by the emblems of the Dominions of which she was now Queen.

Hartnell together with his assistant, Ian Thomas (1929–93) researched each of the emblems in consultation with the Earl Marshal and others, and took them to his embroidery workrooms to be worked up into samples. Trials in the embroidery workroom at Hartnell's headquarters in Bruton Street, London, showed that the coloured silks would form the perfect foundation for each emblem; jewels, sequins and beads would be added as highlights. This combination of pastel colours and rich encrustation is one of the most notable features of the Coronation Dress.

The embroidery was carried out under the direction of Miss Edie Dulie, head of the embroidery workroom. The final design for the dress and the

(above)
Details of the embroidery from the Coronation Dress, Norman Hartnell, 1953

(facing)
The Coronation Dress, showing the crinoline skirt with its three scalloped tiers including leek, shamrock and thistle and broad band of embroidery around the skirt incorporating the emblems of the Commonwealth, 1953

embroidery scheme was selected by the end of October 1952, when, according to Hartnell, he presented The Queen at Sandringham House with the final finished sketch of the dress, together with the embroidery samples for each of the thirteen emblems in gilded wooden frames.

The silk for the Coronation Dress was produced at Lady Hart Dyke's silk farm at Lullingstone in Kent. This farm had also supplied the silk for Queen Elizabeth's coronation dress and robe in 1937, for the robes worn by

(left)
Norman Hartnell
presenting his finished
design to the press on
1 June, 1953

(right)
Norman Hartnell
in his Bruton Street
design studio, 1953

Princesses Elizabeth and Margaret Rose to their parents' coronation, and also for Princess Elizabeth's wedding dress in 1947.

The silk was woven by Warner & Sons of Braintree in Essex. Mr Goodale, the Managing Director, had written to offer the company's services. Warner & Sons had been fortunate to weave the silks and velvets for the 1937 coronation and now wished to be entrusted with 'this most important of tasks', reassuring the Queen's Private Secretary that the requisite skills were still present within the firm's workforce.

The embroideries of the dress, in coloured silks and gold and silver thread, were arranged in three scalloped, graduating tiers that fell from the slightly pointed waist. Each tier, together with the edge of the skirt, the inverted 'V' of the short sleeves and the front and back of the neckline, was bordered with alternating lines of gold bugle beads, diamantes and pearls. The technique for transposing the embroidery design to the fabric was done by tracing the design onto tracing paper, placing the tracing paper on the fabric and pouncing (pricking through the tracing paper with a pouncing machine) onto the fabric. The pricked design was then drawn over with pencil.

The skirt has a slight train and was constructed with a backing of cream taffeta reinforced with horsehair crinoline – a woven fabric made of a mixture of linen and horsehair. This ensured that the skirt would not lose its shape under the great weight of the encrusted embroideries, a technical difficulty that the First Hand, Madame Isabelle, who was in charge of making the dress, had encountered. In the event, the special construction ensured that this difficulty was overcome and the skirt retained its elegant shape. Cecil Beaton, on watching The Queen processing down the aisle of Westminster Abbey, described it thus in his diaries: '… as she walks she allows her heavy skirt to swing backwards and forwards in a beautiful rhythmic effect'.

Thanks to both its design and its construction, Hartnell's Coronation Dress was widely recognised as a triumph on Coronation Day itself and, since then, has been rightly recognised as his masterpiece of royal couture. His experience of designing costumes for the theatre had paid off, for the dress looked perfect under the battery of television lights that filled the Abbey. What is more, the language of emblems of the dress, freshly reinvented from the earlier twentieth-century coronation gowns of Queen Mary (1911) and Queen Elizabeth (1937), subtly encapsulated the changes since 1937 in the composition of the Empire and the evolution of the Commonwealth.

There was huge anticipation surrounding the design of both The Queen's Coronation Dress and her Robe of Estate, and Hartnell was permitted to reveal the designs to the press the day before the Coronation itself. One further garment supplied by Hartnell was the voluminous white linen pleated dress, which The Queen wore over her Coronation Dress for the sacred moment of the Anointing.

The Coronation Robe

At first, The Queen considered wearing the purple Robe of Estate used by her father King George VI, but in the event, she decided on a new one. A new crimson Parliamentary Robe was also commissioned for the Coronation. In the summer of 1952, The Queen, accompanied by Queen Mary, visited the

Museum of London, then located at Kensington Palace to see the historic coronation robes on display as a reminder of what her predecessors had worn.

Both Hartnell and the firm of Wilkinsons submitted requests to be permitted to design and make the Robe of Estate but in the end, the order for the Robe of Estate and Parliamentary Robe was awarded to Ede and Ravenscroft of Chancery Lane. The embroidery was to be designed and made by the Royal School of Needlework.

Ede and Ravenscroft's quotations, dated December 1952, detail the following specifications for the Parliamentary Robe: 'to making a parliamentary robe in the best quality hand-made velvet, trimmed with best quality Canadian ermine and gold lace in the traditional manner', and for the Robe of Estate: 'to making and supplying a coronation robe for Her Majesty Queen Elizabeth II in the same shape as the robe of Her Majesty Queen Elizabeth The Queen Mother in best quality hand-made purple velvet trimmed with best quality Canadian ermine 5" on top and under side and fully lined with pure silk English satin, complete with ermine cape all being tailed ermine in the traditional manner and including the embroidery charge of the Royal School of Needlework.'

There had been concern that it would not be possible to obtain the material required to make both new robes but this did not prove to be the case. The raw silk for the velvet for them was supplied, like that for the Coronation Dress, by Lady Hart Dyke's silk farm at Lullingstone in Kent and the fine silk velvet was woven, like the silk for the Coronation Dress, by Warner & Sons, on a handloom in two 18-metre lengths, each measuring 53 centimetres wide.

Ede and Ravenscroft initially included with their estimate a design for satin kirtles, or surcoats, to be worn over the Coronation Dress and immediately underneath the Parliamentary Robe and the Robe of Estate. In the event, however, The Queen decided not to wear a kirtle and as a result, more of Hartnell's Coronation Dress was visible.

Having decided to order a new Robe of Estate, The Queen was anxious that it should not be plain like the one that her father, King George VI, had

(above)
Embroideress at work on the Coronation Robe, 11 February 1953
RCIN 2002692

(facing)
The Coronation Robe of Queen Elizabeth II, Ede and Ravenscroft, embroidery by the Royal School of Needlework, 1953

worn at his coronation. In November 1952, therefore, The Queen's Lady in Waiting passed on Her Majesty's preferences with regard to the embroidery of the robe to Mrs Hamilton-King, Principal of the Royal School of Needlework. Three designs for the border were submitted and The Queen chose the 'number one' design. The robe was to be plain in the middle and was also to be wider at the apex to give it a rounded rather than a square shape, and instead of working Her Majesty's crowned cipher in capital letters, which would look 'so hard', the letters were to be intertwined. The elegance and restraint of the finished design is of note when compared to the heavily embroidered designs of the queen's consort coronation robes worn by Queen Mary and Queen Elizabeth (see p. 37).

Detail of the border of the Coronation Robe showing wheat ears and olive branches symbolising prosperity and peace, embroidery by the Royal School of Needlework, 1953

The embroidery of The Queen's Robe of Estate was executed in goldwork using 18 different types of gold thread by twelve embroideresses from the Royal School of Needlework and took more than 3,500 hours between March and May 1953. The Royal School of Needlework employed its policy of 'never a seat goes cold', which meant that if an embroideress left the workroom she was immediately replaced. In addition to the crowned ER cipher, they

Coronation Sampler
showing the 18 types of
gold thread used in the
Robe of Estate, worked
by the Royal School of
Needlework, 1953

ROYAL SCHOOL OF NEEDLEWORK.
[FORMERLY MRS. HAMILTON-KING.]
25, PRINCES GATE, KENSINGTON, S.W.7.
KENSINGTON 0670/1.

Smooth Purl

Rough Purl

Bright Check Purl

Dull Check Purl

Large Gold Bullion

Medium Gold Bullion

Smooth Bullion

Bright Check Bullion

Gold Passing

Gold Twist

Spangles

Crinkled Plate

Embossed Plate

Embossed Plate

Large Pearl-Purl
or Bead Purl

Pearl-Purl
or Bead Purl

Twisted Gimp

Twisted Gimp

embroidered the border of wheat ears and olive branches, symbolising prosperity and peace. Permission was given in February 1953 for the robe to be both filmed and photographed while it was being made. A specially made metal trunk to contain the Robe of Estate was also supplied to The Queen by Ede and Ravenscroft, together with one further garment – a mock robe which The Queen used for practice and rehearsals.

The Queen's Jewellery

On Coronation Day, The Queen wore important diamond jewellery that both fitted the occasion and had strong historic references. For the journey to Westminster Abbey, she wore the Diamond Diadem, which was designed and made by Rundell, Bridge & Rundell in 1820 for George IV's coronation the following year. The design incorporates the national emblems of the

The Diamond
Diadem, 1820

The Coronation Necklace
and Earrings, 1858

thistle, rose and shamrock, and includes 1,333 diamonds set in silver and gold. The Queen also wore the Coronation Necklace and Earrings, made in 1858 for Queen Victoria by R&S Garrard & Co. The Coronation Necklace takes its name from having been worn by Queen Alexandra, Queen Mary and Queen Elizabeth at their coronations as queen consort in 1902, 1911 and 1937 respectively. It consists of 25 graduated brilliant diamonds with a pendant drop known as the Lahore Diamond. The Coronation Earrings had also been worn by Queen Mary and Queen Elizabeth on their coronation days.

The Duke of Edinburgh's Uniform

The Duke of Edinburgh wore the Full Dress Uniform of an Admiral of the Fleet with his orders and decorations, including the star, badge and collar of the Order of the Garter and the star of the Order of the Thistle. At the time of the Coronation, the Full Dress Uniform of an Admiral of the Fleet was richly applied with gold-bullion-trimmed epaulettes and gold oak leaves on the collar and sleeves. Subsequent changes in naval dress regulations reduced the amount of gold decoration permitted and as a result His Royal Highness's uniform has since been altered. His robe of red silk velvet trimmed with ermine was made by Ede and Ravenscroft, who also made his silver-gilt ducal coronet.

(facing)
The Duke of Edinburgh's uniform of an Admiral of the Fleet, Coronation Robe and coronet

(above)
HRH The Duke of Edinburgh, Cecil Beaton, 2 June 1953
RCIN 2507923.M

(right)
The Duke of Edinburgh's bicorn hat and epaulettes, 1953

The Dresses of the Maids of Honour

Norman Hartnell's involvement with the Coronation was not limited to The Queen's Coronation Dress. He was also responsible for designing the dresses worn by all the principal ladies of the immediate Royal Family, together with those for the Maids of Honour. Having been asked to create this complete collection of dresses, Hartnell was able to produce a coherence of style that gave a remarkably unified effect, whether the onlooker was witnessing the Coronation in Westminster Abbey or watching it on television.

Hartnell paid particular attention to the dresses worn by the six Maids of Honour – Lady Jane Vane-Tempest-Stewart, Lady Anne Coke, Lady Moyra Hamilton, Lady Mary Baillie-Hamilton, Lady Jane Heathcote Drummond

(below)
Queen Elizabeth II with her Maids of Honour, Cecil Beaton, 2 June 1953

(facing left)
Detail showing the application of the embroidery

(facing right)
The back of the Maid's of Honour dress showing the embroidery which falls down the centre to the hemline, Norman Hartnell, 1953

Willoughby and Lady Rosemary Spencer-Churchill. The design was adapted from one Hartnell had already prepared for that season's collection, entitled *Silver and Gold*. However, he gave the design his customary careful thought and added signature embroideries in a restrained colour palette which harmonised with those of the other royal Coronation clothes. As a result, the Maids of Honour, with their long white silk gloves and halo-shaped headdresses, created a truly elegant, almost ethereal vision.

The First Hand, Madame Alice, was in charge of the workroom and was tasked with making the dresses. As Mrs Ann Wright, who worked under Madame Alice, recalls, the patterns were built up from the initial sketch but a separate toile was necessary for each dress in order to give the Maids of Honour a uniformity of scale and proportion, despite their differing heights.

Hartnell was acutely aware that their dresses would be scrutinised from all angles but most particularly from the back, since the Maids of Honour followed behind The Queen, carrying her robes in procession along the aisle of Westminster Abbey. As he recalled in his autobiography, he therefore planned 'for the embroideries of small gold leaves and pearl white blossom to cascade down the backs of their billowing skirts of white satin'.

The dresses were made of cream silk satin and were edged around the V-shaped neckline and arms with gold tissue. The embroidery, which was applied to both the front and back of the bodice, around the hips and down the centre of the back of the skirt, took the form of trailing flowers and foliage. These were executed in gold bugle beads and silver and gold leaf-shaped beads,

and were highlighted by pearls and diamantes. The dresses had a concealed fastening, which meant that no zips or other closures would be visible from the back. The Maids of Honour also wore headdresses of leaves and flowers in gold and white silk with applied sequins and beads.

The Dress of Queen Elizabeth The Queen Mother

As Queen Elizabeth's principal couturier, Norman Hartnell was the obvious choice to design the ensemble she would wear for her daughter's coronation. Hartnell devised a crinoline-skirted gown in white satin bordered in gold tissue and embroidered with a feather design in crystal, gold and diamante. With this, Queen Elizabeth wore a silk velvet robe trimmed with gold, ermine and lace. Her jewels included Queen Victoria's Diamond Fringe Brooch, the Greville Peardrop Earrings, the family orders, the broad riband and badge of the Order of the Garter, the Duchess of Teck's Collet Necklace and her own diamond Coronation Necklace.

(above left) Queen Elizabeth The Queen Mother with The Duke of Cornwall and Princess Anne, Cecil Beaton, 2 June 1953

(above right) Queen Victoria's Diamond Fringe Brooch, R&S Garrard & Co., 1853

(facing) The Queen Mother's dress and detail of the feather embroidery design, Norman Hartnell, 1953

(facing)
Princess Margaret's dress,
Norman Hartnell,
and robe, Ede and
Ravenscroft, 1953

(below left)
Detail of the dress
embroidery

(below right)
The Diamond Halo
Tiara, Cartier, 1936

Despite the overall scheme of white and gold worn by the royal ladies, Hartnell was nonetheless adept at giving each dress its appropriate importance and making it distinct from the others. For Princess Margaret he conceived a dress of white satin with an openwork design of *broderie anglaise*. It also had crystal embroideries applied in a design of stylised marguerites and roses – a reference to her name Margaret Rose – and highlighted with silver thread and pearls. Princess Margaret was later to alter the appearance of her dress by removing the sleeves, thereby allowing it to be worn on other occasions.

Princess Margaret also wore a robe of purple velvet and ermine and a princess's coronet made by Ede and Ravenscroft, together with the Cartier Halo Tiara, which had been loaned to her by The Queen.

The Outfits worn by Prince Charles and Princess Anne

For the four-year-old Prince Charles, Duke of Cornwall and two-year-old Princess Anne, specially designed clothes were ordered from the children's outfitters, Miss Hodgson of 33 Sloane Street, London. The Duke of Cornwall, who attended part of the Coronation Ceremony, wore a cream silk shirt with a lace jabot and lace-trimmed cuffs, a silk sash, cream woollen trousers and page's shoes. He also wore his Coronation Medal.

Princess Anne, who was considered too young to attend the ceremony but who excitedly took part in waving off her parents as they departed for the Abbey and was captured in charming detail in some of the more informal portraits taken by Cecil Beaton, wore a cream silk and lace dress with a scalloped hem, a silk sash with a bow at the back, and matching cream silk ballet shoes. To complete her outfit she wore a gold and ruby brooch and a pearl and gold necklace.

Hartnell also designed dresses for two other members of the Royal Family, the Duchess of Kent and her daughter, Princess Alexandra, as well as for the

Ladies of the Bedchamber. For the Duchess of Kent, he designed a dress of white satin with panels of embroidery, and for Princess Alexandra, a dress of white lace and tulle threaded with gold.

Rules of Dress for those Attending the Coronation

A sub-committee of the Coronation Committee was formed to consider the matter of dress for those attending or taking part in the ceremony. This committee was mindful of the shortages of certain materials so they made some modifications to the rules of dress laid down for the 1937 coronation.

The revised rules of dress were issued by the Earl Marshal in December 1952. Those in procession inside the Abbey would either wear Full Dress Uniform or one of the forms of court dress laid down in the Lord Chamberlain's Regulations for Dress at Court. Knights Grand Cross, Knights Grand Commander and Officers of the Orders of Knighthood, except those attending in another capacity, would wear the mantles of their orders, and the Kings of Arms of the Orders would require their crowns. Collingwood, the jewellers, undertook the regilding and relining of certain of the crowns for the Kings of Arms, including those for the Order of the Bath and the Order of St Michael and St George.

The dress requirements for the various grades of civil service, foreign office civilian, colonial office and officers in the services were also carefully set out. Ladies were to wear evening or afternoon dresses with a light veiling falling from the back of the head. No hats or coats could be worn but a light wrap was permissible. Dames Grand Cross would wear the mantles of their orders and were entitled also to wear tiaras.

The dress regulations for peers and peeresses were more complex. Peers taking part in the processions or ceremonies were to wear Robes of State with coronets over full dress civil or military uniform. Otherwise they were to wear robes over full velvet court dress. Those peers who were not taking part in the processions or ceremonies were expected to wear the same dress as the rest of the peerage if possible, or could wear the mantles of the Orders of Knighthood to which they were entitled or any dress worn at a previous coronation.

Velvet court dress for gentlemen in 1953 was of two types, either old style or new style. The two differed in small details, such as the number of buttons; both were permissible at the Coronation. The complete court dress, whether

(facing, clockwise)
Robe and coronet for
a peer over old-style
court dress

Robe, kirtle and coronet
of a peeress

The coronets of an earl,
a baron and a countess,
made by Garrards for
the Coronation, 1953

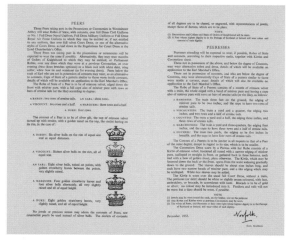

(left)
Design for
a peeress's robe,
Norman Hartnell, 1952

(right)
The Earl Marshal's
Orders Concerning the
Robes and Dress to
be worn by Peers and
Peeresses

RA LC-LCO-MAIN-583-1953

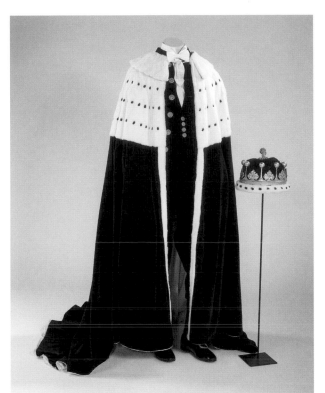

old or new style, comprised a black silk velvet coat, a white satin or black silk velvet waistcoat, black silk velvet breeches, black silk hose, black patent leather shoes, black beaver cocked hat, evening dress shirt with winged collar, white bow neck tie, white gloves and a sword.

Peeresses were expected to wear Robes of State and coronets according to their rank, together with kirtles and coronation dress. Those who were not in possession of robes, coronets and coronation dress, and who were below the rank of countess, could wear alternative robes and dress. Norman Hartnell supplied designs for this alternative dress and his designs were approved by the Earl Marshal who included them in his regulations.

The robes and coronets worn by peers and peeresses differed in their design and size, according to the rank of the wearer. The Robe of State of a peer was of crimson velvet edged with miniver pure (the white belly fur of Baltic

(left)
Eight peers in robes and coronets processing, Feliks Topolski, 1953
RCIN 926363

(right)
Peers in the abbey, Feliks Topolski, 1953
RCIN 926365

(left)
The Earl Marshal's robe,
coronet, coatee, breeches
and baton

(right)
Garter King of Arms,
breeches, tabard, crown
and sceptre

squirrels), with a cape with rows of ermine tails, the number of which varied according to rank. A baron had two rows of tails, a viscount two and a half, an earl three, a marquess three and a half, and a duke four. Correspondingly, peers' coronets also varied according to degree. Peeresses' robes and coronets were also distinguishable according to the rank of the wearer. In the case of the robes, the length of the train and the number of rows of ermine tails gave an indication. A baroness's train was to be three feet (90 cm) on the ground, while a duchess's was to be two yards (180 cm).

The specification for a peeress's full court dress worn beneath the robe and kirtle was most precise. The dress should be of 'white or slightly cream colour with lace, embroidery or brocade in accordance with taste' and 'feathers and veils will not be worn but a tiara should be worn if possible'. Unsurprisingly,

London jewellers were at a peak of activity in the run up to the Coronation, repairing, renovating and supplying tiaras.

The dress of the peers and peeresses was part of the great spectacle of Coronation Day. Many records of the day, both visual and written, capture their elegance. Hartnell, from his seat in Westminster Abbey, likened the scene to a sumptuous tea party: '… opposite are row upon row of peeresses mounting towards the very roof. They look like a lovely hunk of fruit cake; the damson jam of the velvet bordered with the clotted cream of ermine and sprinkled

(left)
Livery of a Royal Page
of Honour

(right)
Livery of a Page of a Peer,
worn at the Coronation

The Archbishop
of Canterbury,
Dr Geoffrey Fisher,
wearing the cope and
mitre worn at the
Coronation, 1953

with the sugar of diamonds' and '… the peers attired in their masculine version of ermine and velvet, their jam puff coronets nestling in their laps.'

The colour and movement of the peers' robes was captured in one of Feliks Topolski's (1907–89) preparatory sketches for his Coronation Frieze commissioned by the Duke of Edinburgh in 1959 (see p. 68).

Each member of the Royal Family was attended by pages, as was each peer and peeress. The royal pages wore the traditional livery of a red tunic with white silk breeches, while the pages of the peers and peeresses wore their family liveries. All contributed to the jewel-like appearance of the interior of the Abbey.

Another distinctive figure captured by Topolski in his frieze was the fleetingly observed Archbishop of Canterbury, Dr Geoffrey Fisher. However, Topolski's sketch does not provide any indication of the extraordinary richness of the Archbishop's embroidered cope. The cope and mitre were presented to Archbishop Fisher in 1948 by Bishop Yashiro of Japan. They were made of Japanese silk and brocade by craftsmen of the Brotherhood of St Andrew.

The other most senior figures attending the Coronation wore the uniforms of their Offices of State. The Earl Marshal wore court dress consisting of a coatee, breeches, ducal robes and a ducal coronet, together with his baton of office. Garter King of Arms wore his tabard and crown (see p. 69).

SPLENDOUR and CEREMONY

Coronation Day

Tuesday, 2 June 1953 dawned cold and wet. However, this did not seem to dampen the spirits of the thousands of people who had slept out overnight, some for two nights in succession, along the processional route. They were keen to ensure they had a glimpse of the newly-crowned Queen and the splendour of the Coronation procession. The nation also awoke that day to the news that the British expedition led by Edmund Hillary (1919–2008), was the first to have conquered Mount Everest.

Hours of preparation for the Coronation had already been underway long before daylight as troops, horses, carriages and regalia were made ready. The 8,251 guests from 129 countries and territories were to be admitted to Westminster Abbey from 6:00 in the morning and had to be seated before 8:30, when the Abbey doors were closed. They had a long wait ahead, for the service would not commence until 11:15 and would last three hours, but many had come prepared with picnics, sweets and hip flasks to sustain them.

Those seated in the specially constructed stands lining The Mall close to Queen Victoria's Monument were fortunate to see the carriage processions arriving from the Royal Mews and departing from Buckingham Palace for the Abbey. The first carriage procession to depart from the Palace was that of the colonial rulers, including the Queen of Tonga and the Sultan of Kelantan. Next, leaving at 9:20, came the procession of prime ministers of the Dominions, led by the carriage occupied by Sir Winston and Lady Churchill. At 9:40 the procession of members of the Royal Family began to depart with an escort of the Household Cavalry, and at 10:00 Queen Elizabeth The Queen Mother and Princess Margaret departed together from Clarence House.

At 10:26 precisely, the fifth and final carriage procession – the Queen's procession, with a Sovereign's Escort of the Household Cavalry – departed. The Queen and The Duke of Edinburgh travelled in the Gold State Coach drawn by eight Windsor Greys. These were followed by two State Landaus conveying two of the Maids of Honour and senior members of The Queen's Household. These included the Mistress of the Robes, the Lord Chamberlain and the Private Secretary.

The Gold State Coach, designed by William Chambers (1723–96), was first used for the State Opening of Parliament by George III in 1762. It has been used to convey the Sovereign to all coronations since that of George IV in 1821. The coach is made of gilded wood with applied panels painted by Giovanni Cipriani that were relined and remounted before the 1953 Coronation. Other work was also carried out in readiness by the coachbuilders Hooper & Co.,

who added rubber tyres, and made fitted receptacles in the velvet- and satin-lined interior to hold the Sovereign's Orb and Sceptre.

The staff of the Royal Mews at Buckingham Palace, where all the carriages and horses in royal use are kept, worked for many months in preparation for the Coronation. Repairs and renovations were carried out to the state harness, new state liveries were ordered, and new rosettes, and an abundance of streamers and hairbows for the horses were acquired from the horse milliners H.E. Davies.

On the drive to Westminster Abbey, The Queen carried the Coronation Bouquet, which had been presented by the Worshipful Company of Gardeners and made by Mr Martin Longman. This white bouquet comprised orchids and lily-of-the-valley from England, stephanotis from Scotland, carnations from Northern Ireland and the Isle of Man, and additional orchids from Wales. A bouquet was also presented for The Queen's state drive to the Guildhall after the Coronation, on 12 June.

The Coronation Bouquet,
Anna Zinkeisen, 1953
RCIN 407248

Arrival at Westminster Abbey

The Queen, holding the
Coronation Bouquet, and
The Duke of Edinburgh in the
Gold State Coach on their way
to Westminster Abbey for the
Coronation, 2 June 1953
RCIN 2002755

On arrival at Westminster Abbey the series of grand processions began to enter the church, commencing with the procession of members of the Royal Family, the procession of royal and other representatives of foreign states, the procession of rulers of states under Her Majesty's protection, the procession of the Dean and prebendaries of Westminster Abbey, the procession of the princes and princesses of the blood royal, and the procession of Queen Elizabeth The Queen Mother and Princess Margaret.

The Queen flanked by
the Bishop of Durham
and the Bishop of Bath
and Wells processes into
Westminster Abbey,
2 June 1953
RCIN 2584764

At 10:38 the delivery of the regalia took place, with each component being presented by the Lord Great Chamberlain to the peers appointed to bear it in procession. The Queen and The Duke of Edinburgh arrived at the Abbey at 11 o'clock then retired briefly to allow those taking part in Her Majesty's procession to form up in their places in the vestibule. At 11:15, the procession of Her Majesty The Queen, which numbered some 250 representatives of Crown, Church and State, proceeded in state from the west door, leading The Queen to her Chair of Estate near the altar to the accompaniment of Sir Hubert Parry's *I Was Glad*.

Preceding The Duke of Edinburgh in The Queen's procession was the Archbishop of Canterbury with the primatial cross of Canterbury carried before him.

Those attending the Coronation service followed it by using the *Form and Order of the Service*. The Queen signed the copy that she used on the day and placed it in the Royal Library at Windsor Castle.

The Chair of Estate, in which The Queen sat at the start of the service, was made by the firm of White & Allom. After the Coronation it was sent to Buckingham Palace, where it was placed in the Throne Room, together with a companion chair for The Duke of Edinburgh, which was made after the Coronation.

The faldstools used by The Queen and The Duke of Edinburgh were retained at Westminster Abbey and have been used on subsequent occasions, including at the wedding of The Duke and Duchess of Cambridge in April 2011.

The Recognition

The first stage of the Coronation was the Recognition. During this stage, the Archbishop of Canterbury, the Lord Chancellor, the Lord Great Chamberlain, the Lord High Constable and the Earl Marshal with Garter King of Arms preceding them went to the east, south, west and north sides of the Coronation Theatre. Here they presented The Queen, who, having arisen from the Chair of Estate, likewise turned to the four sides as they asked the congregation to recognise her as their monarch. The congregation responded by proclaiming, 'God Save Queen Elizabeth'.

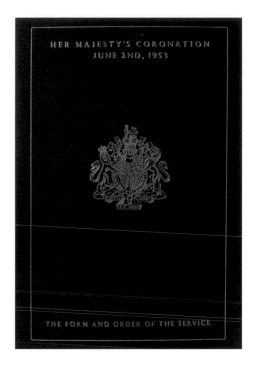

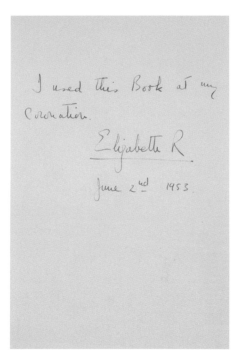

I used this Book at my Coronation.

Elizabeth R

June 2nd 1953

The Queen's bound copy of the Form and Order of the Service, 1953
RCIN 1006834

For the second stage of the Coronation, the Oath, The Queen, having given her responses to the Archbishop in which she promised to take the Oath, govern the people and use Law, Justice and Mercy to be executed in her judgements and defend the faith, proceeded to the altar to sign the Oath. This was made of vellum 'roughened for the signature'. Its production had been the responsibility of John Hunt, Clerk of the Chamber of the House of Lords. The Queen signed the Oath using a specially made pen, which had been offered by the Worshipful Company of Scriveners on 23 December 1952. The

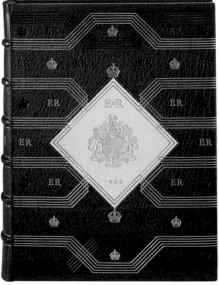

pen was in the form of a conventionalised feather, with the vane made of ivory and the shaft and decoration of gold. The rib of the quill is a representation of the Sword of State, which is carried before the Sovereign as she proceeds to the altar to sign the transcript of the Oath. Superimposed on the sword was a jewelled crown supported by cherubs, which represented The Duke of Cornwall and Princess Anne. On the hexagonal shaft was the motto of the Worshipful Company of Scriveners – *Litera Scripta Manet* (the written word remains).

(left)
The Coronation Bible being tooled
RCIN 2584742

(right)
The Coronation Bible, 1953
RCIN 108362

Once The Queen was again seated on her Chair of Estate, the Presentation of the Holy Bible took place. For the first time at a coronation, the Moderator of the General Assembly of the Church of Scotland took the role of presenting the Bible to The Queen.

The Coronation Bible used in 1953 was produced by Oxford University Press. The Bible that had been used at the coronation in 1937 had been found to be too heavy so in 1953 a small lectern Bible, intended to be more portable, was printed on India paper. After the Coronation the Bible passed to the Archbishop of Canterbury and today is held at Westminster Abbey. An identical copy to the one on which The Queen took the Oath was presented to The Queen after the Coronation. The binding was designed by Lynton Lamb and executed by Sangorski & Sutcliffe.

The Coronation
Pen used by The Queen
to sign the Oath
RCIN 39431

The most sacred part of the Coronation service – the Anointing – effectively consecrates the Sovereign and sets them apart from the people. This mystical ritual was the only part of the Coronation service that was neither televised nor photographed. While the Anointing was in progress, the choirs and musicians performed Handel's anthem *Zadok the Priest*.

In readiness for the ceremony, The Queen was divested of all symbols of her status – her Parliamentary robe, the Diamond Diadem and the Coronation Necklace – by the Lord Great Chamberlain assisted by the Mistress of the Robes. She was then dressed in a simple white pleated dress designed by Norman Hartnell intended to show the monarch 'uncovered' in a state of humility without the trappings of kingship. The Queen was then seated in

(facing)
The Queen seated beneath
the Anointing Canopy
RCIN 2584765

(left)
Detail of the pleated linen dress
worn during the Anointing,
Norman Hartnell, 1953

(below)
The Anointing Canopy (detail).
The canopy conceals the sacred act of
Anointing from the public gaze and
is embroidered with Imperial Eagles,
Royal School of Needlework, 1937

St Edward's Chair, otherwise known as the Coronation Chair. This was made to the orders of King Edward I in 1300–01 and almost every monarch since Edward II in 1308 has been crowned in it.

During the Anointing, four Knights of the Garter carried forward on wooden and silver poles the Anointing Canopy. The canopy was made for the coronation of King George VI in 1937 woven from cloth of gold by Warner & Sons and embroidered by the Royal School of Needlework. Having been sent on exhibition after the 1937 coronation, the poles were damaged, so silver bands were applied in May 1953 to strengthen them. The canopy itself also required some repairs, which were carried out by the Royal School of Needlework, and one of the four original silver-thread tassels from the corners had been lost, so the Goldsmiths and Silversmiths Company (later Garrard & Co.) supplied a replacement.

The Queen was then anointed with holy oil on the hands, breast and head by the Archbishop of Canterbury. The holy oil contained oils of orange, roses, cinnamon, musk and ambergris, and was applied using the Ampulla – a gold ornamental flask in the form of an eagle – and the Coronation Spoon – the only relic to survive from the medieval regalia.

The Ampulla (right), Robert Vyner, 1661, and the Coronation Spoon (left), twelfth century
RCINS 31732, 31733

The Queen is presented with
the Sovereign's Orb by the
Archbishop of Canterbury
RCIN 2002738

During the Investiture the sovereign is presented with the symbols of
sovereignty. In readiness for the Investiture, The Queen was dressed in the
Colobium Sindonis, a plain white garment newly made for each coronation
and, in 1953, supplied by Ede and Ravenscroft. Over this was placed the
Supertunica made for the coronation of George V in 1911. This was fastened
with the Girdle, which was made by the Worshipful Company of Girdlers and
presented to The Queen in 1953.

The first symbols of sovereignty with which The Queen was presented were the Spurs followed by the Jewelled Sword of Offering. Its scabbard incorporates a design of roses, thistles and shamrocks set with precious stones.

Next, the Archbishop placed the Armills on The Queen's wrists. These are bracelets made of gold that represent sincerity and wisdom. Those used in 1953 were a present to The Queen from the Commonwealth countries on the occasion of her Coronation.

The Jewelled Sword of Offering made for George IV's coronation in 1821, Rundell, Bridge & Rundell
RCIN 31726

The Spurs, Rundell, Bridge & Rundell, 1661
RCIN 31725

The Armills, Garrard & Co., 1953
RCIN 31724

(facing)
Imperial Mantle
RCIN 31794

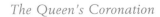

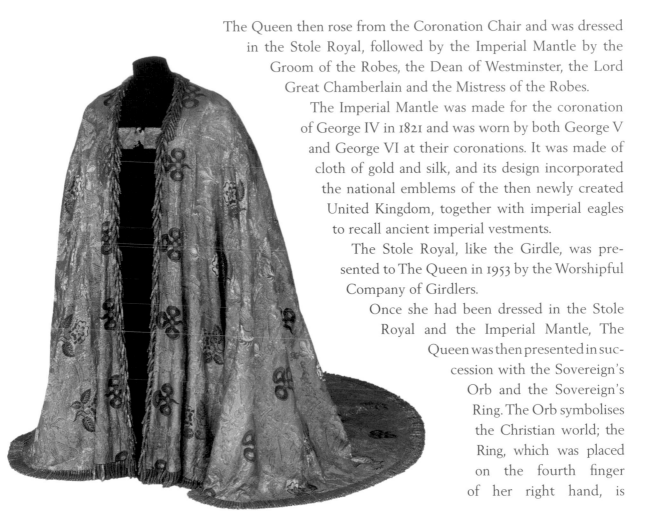

The Queen then rose from the Coronation Chair and was dressed in the Stole Royal, followed by the Imperial Mantle by the Groom of the Robes, the Dean of Westminster, the Lord Great Chamberlain and the Mistress of the Robes.

The Imperial Mantle was made for the coronation of George IV in 1821 and was worn by both George V and George VI at their coronations. It was made of cloth of gold and silk, and its design incorporated the national emblems of the then newly created United Kingdom, together with imperial eagles to recall ancient imperial vestments.

The Stole Royal, like the Girdle, was presented to The Queen in 1953 by the Worshipful Company of Girdlers.

Once she had been dressed in the Stole Royal and the Imperial Mantle, The Queen was then presented in succession with the Sovereign's Orb and the Sovereign's Ring. The Orb symbolises the Christian world; the Ring, which was placed on the fourth finger of her right hand, is

set with diamonds surrounding a sapphire set with the cross of St George in rubies, which represent dignity.

The regalia were carefully cleaned and prepared before the Coronation by Garrard's. Their work included some minor alterations, including adjustment of the ring to fit The Queen's finger.

After putting on the Sovereign's Ring, the Queen was presented with the Coronation Glove. This was specially made for The Queen by the Worshipful Company of Glovers, who presented it to the Lord Chamberlain on 22 May 1953 in an oak case made from the timbers of HMS *Victory*. The case was lined with the same purple silk velvet that had been used to make The Queen's Robe of Estate. The Coronation Glove of white leather was embroidered in

gold thread with the English, Scottish, Welsh and Irish emblems and with The Queen's crowned cipher. In accordance with tradition, the Coronation Glove was returned to the donors after the Coronation.

Having been presented with the Coronation Glove, the Archbishop of Canterbury delivered the Sovereign's Sceptre, or Sceptre with Cross, into The Queen's right hand and the Sceptre with Dove into her left hand.

The most momentous part of the Coronation service – the Crowning – was then about to take place. The congregation all stood while the Archbishop of Canterbury

(facing)
St Edward's Crown, 1661
RCIN 31700

(above)
The moment of Crowning
RCIN 2584766

took St Edward's Crown from the altar. Assisted by the other bishops, the Archbishop then went to the Coronation Chair and, taking the crown from the Dean of Westminster the Archbishop placed it upon The Queen's head.

St Edward's Crown was made for the coronation of Charles II in 1661 and is only ever used for the act of crowning a new monarch. A new purple velvet cap trimmed with ermine was made by Garrard's to fit inside it for The Queen's Coronation.

At the sight of the crowning at exactly 12:33, the Acclamation of the Crowning took place. This involved all those present shouting 'God Save The Queen' while the princes and princesses, and the peers and peeresses simultaneously put on their coronets, and the Kings of Arms their crowns. The Acclamation was also marked by the State Trumpeters playing a fanfare, a gun salute being fired from the Tower of London and a peel of bells being rung at Westminster Abbey.

The Homage

Once the Investiture was completed, The Queen was enthroned in her Throne Chair by the Archbishop and the bishops. Around her stood the peers, the great officers, and those who had carried the regalia. This was the moment for the Homage to begin, when the Church and the aristocracy pledge their loyalty to the Sovereign. For this act the peers removed their coronets, knelt in turn in front of The Queen on a small stool, placed both hands between The Queen's and repeated their pledge of loyalty before touching the crown and kissing The Queen's left cheek.

(below)
The Throne Chair,
White Allom & Co., 1953
RCIN 35369

(facing)
The Duke of Edinburgh
paying Homage to
The Queen

The display of the plate beneath the Royal Gallery, 2 June 1953

Altar dish with a scene of the Last Supper, Henry Greenway, 1664
RCIN 31745

Then came the final part of the Coronation service – the Communion. During this, The Queen made her Oblation – an offering to the Archbishop of Canterbury of an altar cloth and a gold ingot of 500 grams in weight contained within a velvet bag.

Some of the most magnificent and historic plate from the Royal Collection was used to dress the altar and for the display beneath the Royal Gallery. This included candlesticks, chalices, patens, offertory dishes, flagons, tankards and dishes removed temporarily from the Tower of London, Buckingham Palace and the Chapel Royal, St James's Palace.

Large silk panels embroidered with the Royal Arms were hung on the royal galleries and a smaller panel was placed on the regalia table in the annexe of the Abbey. The large panels were made by Toye & Co. for the coronation of King George VI, while the small panel was made by the firm of Hobson and

Sons (London). A fourth large panel had been planned incorporating the arms of Queen Mary.

During the singing of the *Te Deum*, The Queen left the Coronation Theatre and entered St Edward's Chapel. Here she was disrobed of the Imperial Mantle, the *Supertunica* and the *Colobium Sindonis*. The regalia, including St Edward's Crown, was placed upon the altar. Now dressed in the purple Robe of Estate and wearing the Imperial State Crown (which is the crown the monarch exchanges for St Edward's Crown at the end of the coronation ceremony). The Queen left the chapel and began her procession out of the Abbey as the congregation sang the National Anthem.

The Imperial State Crown was considerably altered by the Goldsmiths and Silversmiths Company so The Queen could wear it. The height was reduced and the outline broadened by changing the shape and curvature of the arches and the angle of the crosses paty and the fleurs de lys. This involved the partial remounting of the lower band of the crown and the entire remounting of the arches. A new silk-lined head fitting was made, together with a new purple velvet cap trimmed with ermine.

The Queen arriving at
Buckingham Palace
RCIN 2002719

(facing, top left)
The coronation procession
approaches Marble Arch,
2 June 1953
RCIN 2584771

(facing, top right)
Crowds cheer as the Gold State
Coach passes by, 2 June 1953
RCIN 2002754

(facing, bottom left)
The Canadian Mounted Police
taking part in the coronation
procession, 2 June 1953
RCIN 2584744

(facing, bottom right)
Commonwealth contingents in
the coronation procession march
down The Mall, 2 June 1953
RCIN 2002645

(following)

The Queen, The Duke of
Edinburgh, The Duke of
Cornwall, Princess Anne, The
Queen Mother and Princess
Margaret make a balcony
appearance on Coronation Day
RCIN 2584772

The service concluded at 2 o'clock in the afternoon and, after lunch in the Abbey annexe, The Queen and The Duke of Edinburgh left Westminster Abbey in the Gold State Coach. They received a rapturous reception from the crowds as they travelled on the processional route around the centre of London, a route that was specially extended to ensure that The Queen could be seen by as many people as possible. Lining the route or taking part in the procession were 29,200 officers, men and women, including 3,600 from the Royal Navy, 16,100 from the Army, 7,000 from the Royal Air Force, 2,000 from the Commonwealth and 500 from the Colonies. The procession stretched for almost three and a half kilometres and took 45 minutes to pass any one given point, taking 2 hours in total.

On arrival at Buckingham Palace, The Queen and The Duke of Edinburgh joined other members of the Royal Family to sit for the official photographic portraits. These were taken by Cecil Beaton in the Green Drawing Room. Large formal group photographs of the extended Royal Family were taken more or less simultaneously in the Throne Room by a photographer from *The Times*.

Then, around an hour later, came the balcony appearance in front of the crowds of hundreds of thousands who lined The Mall and the area in front of the Palace. The members of the Royal Family on the balcony witnessed the fly past by the Royal Air Force.

Further balcony appearances followed, concluding when The Queen with The Duke of Edinburgh turned on the illuminations in The Mall. Floodlighting

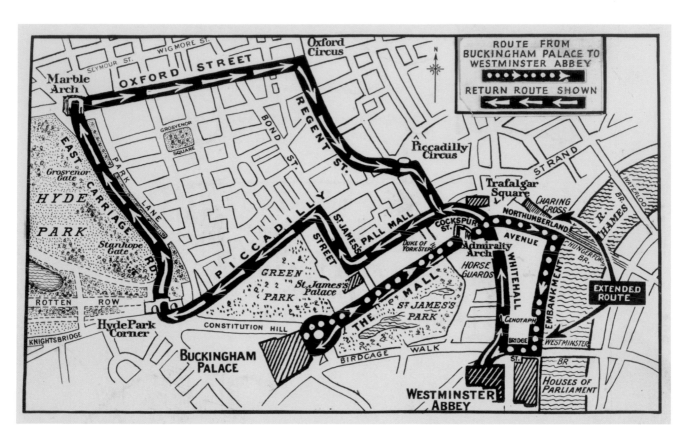

Map of the processional
route to and from
Westminster Abbey

RCIN 2587039

of Buckingham Palace, Windsor Castle, St James's Palace and Hampton Court Palace to celebrate the Coronation continued until 21 June and was extended even further at Windsor Castle until 17 August and until 29 September at St James's Palace and Hampton Court.

The celebratory atmosphere of the day continued with a firework display over the Thames, which was enjoyed by many thousands of onlookers. The fireworks included images in lights of The Queen, The Duke of Edinburgh and their children.

The crowds in The Mall witness the illuminations, 2 June 1953
RCIN 2002620

Fireworks over the
Thames, 2 June 1953
RCIN 2002708

The final task that awaited The Queen on the evening of Coronation Day was to make a broadcast reflecting on the events of the Coronation and thanking the public for its support. This radio broadcast was made live at 9 o'clock in the evening and was relayed around the world. It is regarded as one of the most historic and memorable broadcasts of The Queen's entire reign. In it she declared, 'I have in sincerity pledged myself to your service, as so many of you are pledged to mine. Throughout all my life and with all my heart I shall strive to be worthy of your trust.'

REMEMBERING the DAY

Queen Elizabeth II and
Prince Philip, Duke of
Edinburgh, Cecil Beaton,
2 June 1953

One of the reasons that The Queen's Coronation has stayed so firmly in the public consciousness is no doubt connected to that fact that it was broadcast live by the BBC to many millions of people all over the world. The planning of the operation was immensely complex; it was to be the biggest outside broadcast in the history of the BBC up to that point and would encompass not just radio but also television.

Worldwide interest in the Coronation was taken into account when planning the radio broadcast. The sound team included Commonwealth representatives from Australia, Canada and the West Indies, and the broadcasts were made in 41 languages besides English.

Once concerns about the intrusions of the cameras were allayed and permission was given for the entire service to be televised, the Earl Marshal, the Archbishop of Canterbury and the Minister of Works went to great lengths to ensure the success of the television broadcast. The level of public interest ensured that television sets sold like never before (in fact many people bought their first television specially for the event) and tickets for large-screen showings, for example at London's Festival Hall, sold out within minutes. The 120-strong television team took up their posts around the Coronation route at 7:00 in the morning for what was to be nearly seven hours of broadcasting.

At 10.15 precisely, Sylvia Peters appeared on screen to announce the Coronation broadcast 'on this greatest day in television's history'.

The official portraits, both painted and photographic, made an enormous impact and have left an indelible reminder of The Queen's Coronation. Cecil Beaton's official portrait photographs, all taken in the Green Drawing Room at Buckingham Palace, are among the most enduring ever taken of The Queen. In spite of having photographed the Royal Family from the 1930s onwards, Beaton was, by his own account, surprised to be selected as the official photographer. He was helped in his preparations by being invited to attend the dress rehearsal for the Coronation, which gave him a glimpse of how the Abbey would look. He also spent the day before the Coronation at Buckingham Palace with his assistants, setting up his special backgrounds together with the paraphernalia of cables and lights that would be required.

Beaton's use of theatrical backdrops was a feature of many of his portraits, particularly of royal sitters. For his official Coronation portraits he used a variety of scenes of both the interior and exterior of Westminster Abbey, together with fresh flowers picked from his own garden and arranged in vases from the Picture Gallery at Buckingham Palace.

The Queen on Coronation Day, Cecil Beaton, 2 June 1953

Princess Margaret and Queen Elizabeth, The Queen Mother, Cecil Beaton, 2 June 1953

Queen Elizabeth II on Coronation Day, Cecil Beaton, 2 June 1953

Patrick Matthews, Cecil Beaton and assistants amid studio lights and photographic equipment, Buckingham Palace, 2 June 1953

In his diaries, Beaton describes how, in the act of taking the portraits of The Queen, he had no idea whether they would work or not: 'I was banging away and getting pictures at a great rate; but I had only the foggiest notion of whether I was taking black and white, or colour, or giving the right exposures'. In the event, the portraits selected by The Queen reveal Beaton's carefully thought-out compositions and his perfectly exposed images.

The Queen is seated in a gilded armchair from the Green Drawing Room, wearing the Imperial State Crown and holding the Sovereign's Orb and Sceptre. Behind her an artfully draped curtain reveals the Henry VIII Lady Chapel. The different foreground and background planes create a striking contrast and the low viewpoint means that the viewer's eyeline is on the same level as The Queen's.

In addition to portraits of The Queen and The Duke of Edinburgh, Beaton took group photographs of other members of the Royal Family including Queen Elizabeth The Queen Mother, Princess Margaret, The Duchess of Kent and her family, The Duke and Duchess of Gloucester, and numerous charming, informal images of The Duke of Cornwall and Princess Anne with their grandmother. 'The Queen Mother anchored them in her arms, put her head down to kiss Prince Charles's hair and made a terrific picture', Beaton recalls.

In September 1953 The Queen selected three of Beaton's portraits for presentation. Multiple copies were signed, framed and given to the heads of foreign delegations, ministers and those connected with the Coronation in the United Kingdom, the Maids of Honour, representatives of the Commonwealth countries and the rulers and representatives of the Colonial territories.

Only a small number of painters were permitted to be inside Westminster Abbey for the Coronation. Among these was Terence Cuneo (1907–96), whose painting of the Coronation Theatre depicts The Duke of Edinburgh paying homage to The Queen. Cuneo made a direct request to Buckingham Palace and to Garter King of Arms to paint the Coronation, writing, 'I feel so very strongly that this is a subject which I could really handle'. The Queen gave her permission and subsequent sittings were held with

The Coronation of Queen Elizabeth II,
Westminster Abbey, 2 June 1953,
Terence Tenison Cuneo, 1954
RCIN 404470

Queen Elizabeth II in Coronation Robes,
Sir Herbert James Gunn, 1953–4
RCIN 404386

members of the Royal Family including The Queen and The Duke of Cornwall. The other artists granted a seat in the Abbey were Henry Rushbury, Rodrigo Moynihan and the French artist Maurice Brianchon.

The high viewpoint of Cuneo's picture reflects his location in the Abbey but also creates a sense of drama for the viewer. His painting was presented to The Queen as a gift from Her Majesty's Lord Lieutenants and hangs in Buckingham Palace.

The Queen's State Portrait in Coronation Robes was not completed until 1954. Painted by Sir Herbert James Gunn (1893–1964), it conforms to the tradition of eighteenth- and nineteenth-century state portraits, particularly to those of Queen Alexandra (Sir Luke Fildes) and of Queen Mary (Sir William Llewellyn), in the way it depicts The Queen standing on a dais wearing the Coronation Dress, the Robe of Estate and the Diamond Diadem adjacent to a table bearing the Imperial State Crown and the Sovereign's Sceptre. Gunn had difficulty painting the Coronation Dress, which was retained for him to study after The Queen and The Duke of Edinburgh departed on their Commonwealth Tour in November 1953. It had, however, to be sent out to New Zealand in time for The Queen to wear it for the State Opening of Parliament in Wellington in January 1954.

In 1959 The Duke of Edinburgh commissioned the artist Feliks Topolski to paint a mural commemorating Coronation Day. The mural was specifically commissioned to hang in the Lower Corridor of Buckingham Palace, where it remains on view today. It comprises 14 sections divided into two narratives; one narrative, entitled 'In the Streets', shows various processions on their way

to Westminster Abbey, while the other, entitled 'In the Abbey', depicts the procession out of the Abbey after the Coronation. Topolski's style of narrative painting was well-suited to the subject matter and the mural was based on his own personal impression of the Coronation, which he watched in the streets outside the Abbey having attended the final rehearsal.

As in 1937, exhibitions of the principal dresses, robes and other objects used or worn at the Coronation were planned in its immediate aftermath and proved immensely popular with visitors. A display was mounted in the State Apartments in St James's Palace. A touring exhibition was also organised

for display in Canada, New Zealand and Australia under the auspices of the Central Office of Information and the Commonwealth Relations Office.

Meanwhile, the Coronation festivities continued until the end of July with visits by The Queen and The Duke of Edinburgh around the United Kingdom, providing a welcome opportunity for the nation to see them. On 3, 4, 8 and 9 June, The Queen and The Duke of Edinburgh made official drives through north, south, east and west London. A Coronation Thanksgiving Service was held at St Paul's Cathedral on 9 June, while on 15 June, following long-established coronation tradition, there was a Coronation Fleet Review at Spithead. In addition, The Queen and The Duke of Edinburgh undertook visits to Wales, Scotland and Northern Ireland.

At Buckingham Palace there were two Coronation State Banquets on 3 and 4 June and two evening receptions on 5 and 9 June. These involved a total

Exhibition of Coronation Robes, St James's Palace, 1953
RCIN 2002695

The Queen and The Duke of Edinburgh at the Spithead review, 1953
RCIN 2587099

A view of the Ballroom
set for the Coronation
Banquet, Buckingham
Palace, 3 June 1953
RA MRH-MRH-QEII-FUNC-453-5-5

Menu for the Coronation
State Banquet, 3 June 1953
RA MRH/MRH/QEII/FUNC/453/7

of more than 8,000 guests, including foreign heads of state and representatives and rulers of the Commonwealth countries, as well as the Royal Family.

The origins of the Coronation Banquet, which traditionally took place in Westminster Hall following the monarch's return procession from Westminster Abbey, date back to the earliest recorded feast of the Saxon king Edgar in 973. Many rituals developed around the feast, including the arrival of the King's Champion, for centuries a member of the Dymoke family, who would ride in full armour and throw down his gauntlet three times on behalf of the monarch. The banquet in Westminster Hall was dispensed with at the coronation of William IV but since that date, a celebratory Coronation Banquet has been held at Buckingham Palace.

For The Queen's Coronation in 1953, two banquets were needed in order to accommodate the large number of guests. Each banquet was held in the

Ballroom, with the guests seated at individual round tables and The Queen's rectangular table in the centre of the room. Sèvres porcelain and the finest silver-gilt were used and the floral decorations were conceived by Moyses Stevens and Edward Goodyear. The flowers were specially arranged to suit The Queen's request that both she and The Duke of Edinburgh would be visible to all the guests.

The Coronation was marked in many other remarkable ways including, on 4 July, by the planting of a grove of oak trees in the Great Park at Windsor. Each oak represents one of the Commonwealth countries and there is one each for The Queen and The Duke of Edinburgh.

The Queen ruled that she did not wish to receive personal gifts from foreign and Commonwealth heads of state on the occasion of her Coronation, the exception being from those who had a traditional right to give presents, such as the Sultan of Zanzibar and the Sultan of Brunei. Some gifts, such as the Coronation Glove (see p. 90) and the Coronation Pen (see p. 83), were accepted because of the tradition of their presentation. In addition, a small number of other gifts were accepted, including mangoes from the Prime Minister of India, 100 roses from the organisers of National Rose Week in Canada, a lamprey pie from the City of Gloucester and two magnums of 1848 Armagnac. Many loyal addresses were sent from all over the world and an exhibition of them was held after the Coronation at the Imperial Institute. One of the most significant gifts was from the President and Academicians of the Royal Academy and included works by many leading artists, including Sir Alfred Munnings, Stanley Spencer and Sir James Gunn. Further Royal Academy gifts were presented to

Plan of the grove of oak trees planted in The Great Park, Windsor, 1953
RA PPTO-PP-QEII-COR-CSP-29-6A

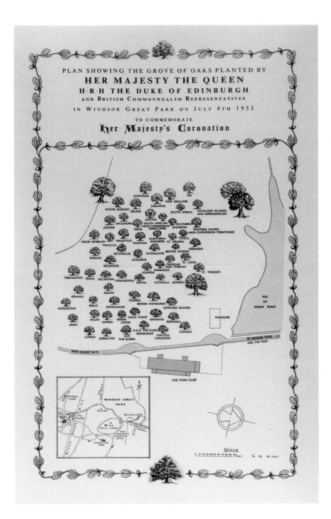

The Queen to mark the Silver Jubilee in 1977 and for the Diamond Jubilee in 2012.

In addition to the signed and framed photographs that The Queen presented to senior figures involved with the Coronation and to heads of state who attended, she made various other gifts. A Coronation Honours list also rewarded those who had played a role in the planning of the Coronation and in the many events constituting the Coronation festivities.

The Queen gave the children of members of staff at the estates of Sandringham, Balmoral and the Crown Estate at Windsor a specially designed Coronation mug and the Maids of Honour were presented with a diamond and platinum brooch in the form of The Queen's cipher, designed and made by Garrards.

Souvenirs to commemorate the Coronation proved extremely popular, not just in the United Kingdom but all over the world. The tradition of coronation souvenirs dates back many centuries. In 1953, owing to difficulties over the supply of metals and the amount of other work the Royal Mint was engaged upon, no official series of commemorative medals was struck for sale to the public as had been the practice for previous coronations. But a Medal Panel and the Coronation Souvenir Committee were established for coronation souvenirs and medals and the Dominions were asked to ensure that all official orders for souvenirs were placed though these crown agents. The Queen Elizabeth II Coronation Medal was issued to commemorate the Coronation and its distribution was arranged through Commonwealth countries and crown dependencies at their discretion. None of the medals was inscribed, with the exception of the 37 that were presented to the members of the British Mount Everest Expedition.

The vast array of souvenirs, examples of which are still found in many homes today throughout the United Kingdom, included souvenir programmes, commemorative china and even models of the Gold State Coach. Queen Mary began a collection of souvenirs to mark her granddaughter's Coronation and today these form part of the Royal Collection.

The anniversary of The Queen's Coronation is marked each year by the flying of flags on government buildings and by the firing of Royal Salutes. Since 1953 significant anniversaries have also been marked by a service at Westminster Abbey. On 4 June 2013, sixty years after Coronation Day, a Service of Thanksgiving was held at Westminster Abbey attended by The Queen, The Duke of Edinburgh and Members of the Royal Family to remember once again an extraordinary day in British history.

The Queen Elizabeth II Coronation medal (obverse)
RCIN 441807

As this day draws to a close, I know that my abiding memory of it will be, not only the solemnity and beauty of the ceremony, but the inspiration of your loyalty and affection.'

Extract from The Queen's Coronation Broadcast to the Nation and the Commonwealth, 2 June 1953

The Queen Elizabeth at Westminster Abbey for the Service of Thanksgiving for the Coronation, June 2003

Chair of Estate		The Queen is seated in the Chair of Estate during the first part of the Coronation ceremony. The Queen's Chair of Estate was made by White & Allom to a seventeenth century design.
Cloth of Gold		A woven fabric made of silk thread wound round with gold wire.
Colobium Sindonis		A simple white vestment in which the sovereign is dressed immediately after the Anointing.
Coronation		The crowning of the sovereign in an ancient ceremony rich in religious significance, historic associations and pageantry. The service, which is always taken by the Archbishop of Canterbury, is based on the fourteenth-century *Liber Regalis*.
Coronation Dress		A dress of sumptuous fabric and decoration worn by female sovereigns or queens consort at the coronation.
Coronation Oath		In the Oath the sovereign swears to govern his or her people according to their respective laws and customs and to preserve true religion. The sovereign also signs the Oath.
Coronation Robe		See Robe of State.
Coronation Robes	*Supertunica*	Also known as the Dalmatic, this is a copy of a Roman consul's dress uniform and is made of cloth of gold. That worn by The Queen in 1953 was originally made for King George V in 1911.
	Girdle	This is used to fasten the *Supertunica* and in 1953 was presented to The Queen by the Worshipful Company of Girdlers.
	Stole Royal	This stole is worn over the *Supertunica* and in 1953 was presented to The Queen by some of the Commonwealth nations.
	Imperial Mantle	Also known as the Pallium Regale, this is worn over the *Supertunica* and represents the four corners of the earth subject to the power of God. It was made for the coronation of George IV in 1821 and is worked with designs of silver coronets, fleurs-de-lis, thistles, shamrocks, roses and imperial eagles, the latter signifying the time when the Saxon King Athelstan was styled 'Emperor of the Kings and people of Britain' in AD 925.

Coronation Theatre	The central space in Westminster Abbey which is created for the coronation ceremony and in which three seats are set for the sovereign's successive occupation – the Chair of Estate is set to the side near the High Altar, St Edward's Chair is set in the middle facing the altar and farther back, approached by five steps is the Throne Chair.
Faldstool	A small upholstered prie-deux at which the sovereign kneels during the coronation ceremony.
Imperial State Crown	The crown worn by the sovereign for the return from Westminster Abbey after the coronation. It is also worn at the State Opening of Parliament.
Robe of Estate	A magnificent robe of purple velvet is worn by the sovereign on leaving Westminster Abbey after the coronation ceremony.
Robe of State	A crimson velvet robe worn by the sovereign on the progress from Buckingham Palace to Westminster Abbey for the coronation and during the first part of the coronation ceremony. It is also worn at the State Opening of Parliament.
St Edward's Chair	Also known as the Coronation Chair this is the chair in which the sovereign is seated for the act of crowning. It was made in 1300 and has been used for every coronation since that time. It is permanently kept in Westminster Abbey.
St Edward's Crown	The coronation crown used purely for the act of crowning the sovereign.
Throne Chair	Also known as the Chair of Homage is the throne to which the newly crowned Queen Elizabeth II moved after the crowning in order to receive homage. Like the Chair of Estate it was made by the firm of White & Allom to a seventeenth-century design.

ACKNOWLEDGEMENTS

The permission of Her Majesty The Queen to reproduce items from the Royal Collection and the Royal Archives is gratefully acknowledged.

In the preparation of this book I have been greatly helped by the generous assistance and expertise of Christopher Allen, Ashley Backhouse, Beatrice Behlen, Rebecca Bissonet, Stephen Brooker, Susanna Brown, the Lady Sarah Chatto, Antonia D'Marco, Jan Faull, the Revd Canon Jonathan Goodall, Rosemary Harden, Dr Jane Hattrick, Sir Stephen Lamport, Maureen Markham, Dr Joanna Marschner, Deborah Phipps, Dr Tony Trowles, Claire Williams and Ann Wright.

The publication of this book would not have been possible without the support of colleagues in Royal Collection Trust and the Royal Household. I gratefully acknowledge the assistance of Hannah Belcher, Virginia Carington, Leslie Chappell, Jacky Colliss Harvey, Lisa Heighway, Paul Hughes, Angela Kelly, Jill Kelsey, Tung Tsin Lam, Karen Lawson, Jonathan Marsden, Theresa-Mary Morton, Daniel Partridge, Shruti Patel, David Rankin-Hunt, Jane Roberts, Alice Ross, Elizabeth Simpson, Stephen Weber, Nick Wright and Eva Zielinska-Millar.

Written by Caroline de Guitaut
Published by Royal Collection Trust / © HM Queen Elizabeth II 2013.

Find out more about the Royal Collection at www.royalcollection.org.uk

ISBN 978 1 905686 80 3
014495

British Library Cataloguing in Publication Data:
A catalogue record of this book is available from the British Library.

Designed by: Paul Sloman
Production by: Debbie Wayment
Colour reproduction by: Altaimage, London
Printed and bound by: Gorenjski tisk
Printed on: Hello Fat 150gsm

page 2 Queen Elizabeth II arrives at Westminster Abbey for her coronation, 2 June 1953
page 4 Detail of embroidery on The Queen's Coronation Dress
All works reproduced are Royal Collection Trust / © HM Queen Elizabeth II 2013 unless indicated below.

Royal Collection Trust is grateful for permission to reproduce the following: Press Association Images pp. 2, 16, 17, 22, 25, 42, 71, 72, 82, 95, 96, 125; Royal Collection Trust/All Rights reserved pp. 6, 8, 11, 51, 60, 61, 86, 88, 90, 91, 92, 103, 107, 109; Trustees of Lambeth Palace Library p. 15; RIBA Library Drawings Collection pp. 20, 21; The Royal Archives pp. 26, 66, 121, 123; Warner Textile Archive, Braintree District Museum Trust Ltd p. 27; Collection of HRH The Prince of Wales p. 30; Royal Collection Trust / © Private Collection pp. 30, 34, 42, 66; Royal School of Needlework pp. 45, 49; Victoria and Albert Museum, London pp. 54, 58, 63, 64, 110, 112, 113, 114, 115; Museum of London, photography Royal Collection Trust / © HM Queen Elizabeth II 2013 pp. 60, 61; Collection of HRH The Duke of Edinburgh, photography Royal Collection Trust / © HM Queen Elizabeth II 2013 pp. 52, 53, 119; © Trustees of Feliks Topolski p. 68; *The Times* p. 87; The Glove Collection Trust, courtesy of the Fashion Museum, Bath and North East Somerset Council p. 90; Crown copyright p. 124.